W9-AGF-985

LIVING FOR THE *FUTURE*

ENERGY
AND
RESOURCES

Paul Brown

W

FRANKLIN WATTS
A Division of Grolier Publishing
NEW YORK • LONDON • HONG KONG • SYDNEY
DANBURY, CONNECTICUT

Most of our everyday activities, whether turning on a light or taking a trip in a car, use up some of the earth's resources. These resources will not last forever, yet we continue to need and use them in our daily lives.

In June 1992, the largest political meeting in history was held — the United Nations Conference on Environment and Development (UNCED), or the "Earth Summit." Politicians, environmental experts, and many others gathered together to discuss the challenge that humanity faces as we move toward the twenty-first century. How can we live our lives in a way that suits us, but without using up the resources that our children will need to live their lives?

Agenda 21 is the document that was produced as a result of the Earth Summit. It sets out a practical plan for every nation to follow to achieve "sustainable development." This means not only allowing us to live the lives we want to lead, but also allowing everyone else to live a comfortable life, while also protecting our environment for future generations.

© 1998 Franklin Watts
First American Edition 1998
by Franklin Watts
A division of Grolier Publishing, Inc.
90 Sherman Turnpike
Danbury CT 06813

Visit Franklin Watts on the Internet at:
http://publishing.grolier.com

Brown, Paul, 1944-
  Energy and resources / Paul Brown. — 1st American ed.
  p. cm. — (Living for the future)
  Includes index.
  Summary: Refers to the aims of the Earth Summit held in June 1992 and to its Agenda 21, a practical plan for every nation to follow to achieve sustainable development.
  ISBN 0-531-14483-6
  1. Energy policy— Juvenile literature. 2. Environmental policy— Juvenile literature. 3. Sustainable development— Juvenile literature. 4. Conservation of natural resources— Juvenile literature. 5. Economic policy— Juvenile literture. [1. Energy resources.] I. Title. II Series.
HD9502.A2B76 1998
333.7'2—dc21   97-34829
                                       CIP AC

Printed in the United Kingdom

Series editor: Helen Lanz   Series designer: Kirstie Billingham
Designer: Simon Borrough   Picture research: Sue Mennell
Consultant: Niall Marriott, a founder of Living Earth Foundation and consultant in environmental, community and educational issues

Picture credits:
Cover images: Main picture: Panos (Nancy Durrell McKenna); Inset: Still Pictures (Mark Edwards)

Inside pictures: Bruce Coleman Ltd. 20m, 21t; James Davis Travel Photography 15b; Ecoscene 10b (Erik Schaffer), 12m (Anthony Cooper), 14m (Peter Holme), 17b (Andrew Brown); Eye Ubiquitous 5t (Keith Mullineaux), 6b (T. Saunders), 16t (Trisha Rafferty), 22m (Graham Wheatley), 26b (Keith Mullineaux); FSC Trademark ©1996 Forest Stewardship Council A.C. (FSC 797/340) 19b; ©1992 GM Corp. Used with permission GM Media Archives 11b; Hutchison Library 9 (Ron Gilling), 10m (Bernard Regent), 12b (Robert Francis), 14b (Tully), 19t (Sue Dent), 22t; Image Bank 12t (Juan Silva); Oxford Scientific Films 21b (Godfrey Merlen); Panos Pictures 6t (Adrian Evans), 7t (Heidi Bradner), 17t (Ron Gilling), 22b (Peter Barker), 23t (Alain le Garsmeur), 27b (Chris Stowers); Popperfoto 8t (Mike Blake); Still Pictures 4t (David Drain), 4b (Mark Edwards), 5b (Hartmut Schwarzbach), 7m (Edward Parker), 7b (Mark Edwards), 8b (Hartmut Schwarzbach), 10t (Mike Jackson), 11t (Thomas Raupach), 14t (Manning-Unep), 16b (Hartmut Schwarzbach), 18t (Michel Gunther), 18m (Mark Edwards), 18b (Daniel Dancer), 20t (Herbert Girardet), 20b (Romano Cagnoni), 22t (Mark Edwards), 22b (Jean-Luc Zeigler), 23b (Mark Edwards), 25t (Thomas Raupach), 25b (Thomas Raupach), 26t (Ray Pfortner), 27t (Thomas Raupach), 28t (Hartmut Schwarzbach), 28b (David Hoffman), 29t (Herbert Girardet), 29b (Julio Etchart); Thames Water 15t; WaterAid 13t (Caroline Penn), 13b (Caroline Penn).

CONTENTS

The water we drink and the air we breathe are essential to keep us alive. Coal, oil, and gas provide energy to keep us warm, and give us fuel for our cars and power for our industries. We burn fuels in power stations to make electricity, which means we can switch on lights and run our refrigerators and washing machines. Wood, brick, and stone are other resources we rely on to build our homes. These are all materials that come from our environment.

New houses use up many natural resources.

ENERGY AND RESOURCES

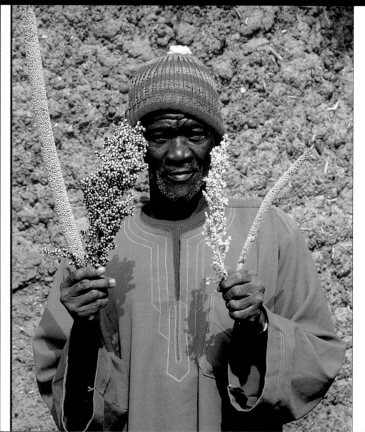

FOOD AND GROWTH

Fertile soil, fresh air, sunshine, and rain, plus water from the earth's rivers and lakes, are the natural resources that plants and trees use to grow. Farmers also rely on these resources to grow crops to provide food for animals and people. But crops are only good to eat if the air, rain, and water are clean. If the air is full of smoke, or the water or soil is polluted, then the crops will be poor or may not grow at all.

A West African farmer displays crops of millet and sorghum grown in a year when the rains were good (left hand), and the same foods when the rains failed (right hand).

GROWTH AND DECAY

Plants have a natural order of new growth at the start of the year and decay at the end of the year. In the autumn, fruits are produced, leaves die, and seeds are scattered; the next year new life begins again. For some plants this whole process takes only one year, but many trees grow very slowly. It can take many years for some trees to be replaced.

Autumn leaves fall, continuing the cycle of growth and decay.

HIDDEN TREASURE

Some natural resources, such as coal and oil, take millions of years to develop. They are the remains of old forests, buried when the earth was young. The trees rotted away, taking on the different forms of coal, oil, and gas. Stored deep underground, they are called fossil fuels.

Coal is used to heat iron ore in a German blast furnace in order to extract the pure metal to make steel.

We have discovered where these deposits of fossil fuels lie and how to dig them up and use them. In a similar way, we dig up chalk and sand to make cement, iron ore to make steel, and silver to make jewelry. There is a constant search for more of these valuable underground treasures.

Until 100 years ago, large parts of the world were still unknown. There were always new places to explore and live. People were surrounded by seemingly plentiful supplies of wood for building, water for drinking, and land for cultivating food.

Rain forests still hold many mysteries.

LIMITED RESOURCES

RUNNING OUT

As recently as the 1960s, people began to realize that there was a limit to the riches of our planet. The forests could not renew themselves as quickly as people could cut them down. In Africa and the Middle East, there was not enough water for the growing populations. Governments across the globe realized that coal, gas, and oil could be running out too. They saw that many resources, once thought of as plentiful, might soon become scarce.

In Nigeria, a Boram woman digs for water for her family in a dry riverbed.

DAMAGE AND POLLUTION

Just as worrisome as resources running out is the damage done to the environment by pollution. Car exhaust and smoke from factories make the air dirty. In places, rain no longer falls as clean water, but contains acid from the smoke, killing trees and damaging buildings. Sewage and chemicals drain into rivers and seas, harming fish and making animals and humans who drink the water sick.

Waste from a chemical factory in Mexico makes this water unusable.

Acid rain caused by pollution from factories has killed this once healthy forest in the former Czechoslovakia.

BRUNDTLAND REPORT

In 1983, because of the concern about resources running out and the damage done by pollution, a World Commission on Environment and Development was set up by the United Nations. The then prime minister of Norway, Mrs. Gro Harlem Brundtland, was in charge. She said the people of the world must change the way they lived. If they did not do so, all the fertile land and forests would be used up. All the coal, oil, and gas would run out. Future generations would have nothing left to live on.

Gro Harlem Brundtland warned that the earth's resources would run out.

In June 1992 many of the world's leaders gathered in Rio de Janeiro, Brazil, at the biggest conference ever held. The United Nations Conference on Environment and Development, the "Earth Summit," was held to try and reach world agreement on limiting the damage being done by people to the environment.

In 1997, Earth Summit II was held to check improvements to the environment.

RESOURCES AND AGENDA 21

Energy-saving technology, such as solar power, must be made available to developing countries.

A PLAN FOR THE FUTURE

All the leaders at the Summit signed an agreement called Agenda 21. This is a practical plan to enable people to live comfortable lives while at the same time making sure that the children of the future do not suffer because people today have used up too many of the world's resources. This is called "sustainable development."

"The Chinese have a proverb: 'If a man cheats the earth, the earth will cheat the man'."

U.S. president George Bush at the Earth Summit.

This plan recognizes the need for countries to invest in industry in order to be able to offer their people a good standard of living. It also recognizes that to solve the world's problems, all nations must work together, sharing knowledge and technology. In this way, each country can develop, while causing as little pollution as possible.

Here are some of the most important aims of Agenda 21 for preserving the earth's resources:

- limit the amount of pollution in the atmosphere and stop the world's climate from heating up too much
- protect fresh water supplies and share what is available
- prevent forests from being destroyed and replant as many trees as possible
- prevent plants and animals from becoming extinct by preserving their habitats
- preserve resources by reusing materials and developing alternative sources of energy from the sun, wind, and water
- stop the spread of deserts

9

CASE STUDY

THE RHINE

SAVING A RIVER

The river Rhine is the largest European river running into the North Sea. Twenty years ago it became so polluted that fish died, and people living along the banks were no longer able to use the water for drinking. The countries the river runs through – Switzerland, France, Germany, and the Netherlands – got together and decided to clean up the water. The river is still not perfect, but nearly all chemical and sewage discharges into the river have been stopped. The fish have returned, and the water can once again be used for drinking.

The cleanup of the Rhine was one of the first successful international plans to save a river.

AGENDA 21 **aims to:**

- clean up the air
- cut down pollution
- slow global warming
- reduce the hole in the ozone layer

Less pollution, fewer illnesses like asthma.

THE AIR WE BREATHE

The earth is warmed by the sun. As sunlight passes through the atmosphere (the gases that surround the earth), it heats up the ground. The heat escapes back into space at night, but how fast it goes depends on the mixture of gases in the air. Air is made up of many gases, such as oxygen and carbon dioxide. If the amount of carbon dioxide is increased, the heat from the ground escapes more slowly and, over time, the earth heats up. Scientists today are concerned that the world is heating up too fast.

Clouds made of water vapor and other gases stop sunshine from reaching the earth but also trap heat near the ground and prevent it from escaping.

A CHANGE IN AIR

When we burn fossil fuels and wood, extra gases, including carbon dioxide, are released into the air through the smoke. These gases trap the earth's heat near its surface, acting like the glass in a greenhouse. Experts have called the resulting warming of the earth "global warming," or the "greenhouse effect." Air pollution also affects people's health, causing asthma and other illnesses.

Black smoke from bonfires, factories, and cars can be a health risk and damage the environment.

A PROTECTIVE LAYER

High in the sky, there is a layer of gas called ozone, which protects the earth from being burned by the sun. This protective layer is being damaged by man-made chemicals that have escaped into the atmosphere from machines such as refrigerators. Holes are appearing in the ozone layer, allowing too much sunshine through, which can cause skin cancer. Now that everyone has realized the danger to the ozone layer, these chemicals are being banned.

Old refrigerators are dumped, but the chemicals used in them can be taken out and recycled to prevent harm to the ozone layer.

"Everyone should have the right to breathe clean air."

AGENDA 21

CASE STUDY

UNITED STATES

LESS FUEL CREATES LESS POLLUTION

Designers at General Motors have built a four-passenger car without using steel, which makes the car lighter. The low weight of the car, combined with its slim sports car design, allows it to use the same amount of fuel as a normal car but to go nearly three times as far.

The need for less fuel not only means preserving resources but also cuts the level of pollution.

AGENDA **21** aims to:

- provide clean water for all
- promote the sharing of water resources
- stop the waste and pollution of water

MANAGING WATER

WATER FOR SURVIVAL

Water is one of our most important resources — we cannot survive without it. Since the beginning of civilization, people have built their homes next to rivers and used water for drinking and cooking. Water also provides power and transportation. Yet the earth's waterways are under constant stress.

In most developed countries, all people have to do to get clean water is to turn on a tap. But even in these countries there is not enough water to meet people's needs.

In the last 50 years, plans to dam rivers have increased: More and more water is taken out of the waterways to meet the needs of growing populations. For example, by the time the great Colorado River in the United States reaches the sea, it is reduced to a trickle. Much of its water has been taken out for the needs of giant cities such as Los Angeles.

(Top) Sprinkler systems to keep gardens beautiful in the summer are wasteful if other people need the water to drink.

(Above right) Bonneville Dam in the United States is just one of eight dams taking water from the Columbia-Snake River.

ACCESS TO WATER

In developing countries, such as Africa and India, access to water is not always straightforward. It is the custom for women in some communities to fetch water for their families. They often have to walk many miles to get enough water for cooking, drinking, and washing. Children sometimes die of disease because the water is dirty and full of germs and viruses. The problem for their mothers is that there is no clean water to give them, but without any water at all, the children will die of thirst.

In Africa, women often walk miles to collect water for their families.

CASE STUDY

AFRICA

A CLEAN SUPPLY OF WATER

In Africa and other countries where industry and technology are not very advanced, people need help to find and use water properly. Organizations such as WaterAid teach people how to dig wells and provide simple pumps to draw the water. Women and their children are taught not to use dirty water for drinking, and waste water is kept away from the clean supplies. Simple, basic sanitation is installed at the same time.

A simple pump to tap underground water makes life much easier in developing countries.

MANAGING SUPPLIES

Governments are sometimes forced to place bans on watering crops in order to save enough water for people to drink and to wash with.

Water needs to be managed and shared carefully, or situations can get out of hand. Problems arise when the people from one country take water that others downstream believe should have been left for their use.

The Nile River in Africa flows through eight countries, all of which need to use water from it. Egypt, the closest to the sea, has the largest army of these countries. Officials have threatened to attack those higher up the river if they use too much water and Egypt does not get its fair share.

> **"Many of the wars of this century were about oil, but wars of the next century will be about water."**
>
> *Ismail Seageldin, Vice President of the World Bank, 1995.*

WATER SHORTAGES

Proper water management means that a country can benefit from its rainfall year-round. By collecting the winter rainfall and stopping it from running into the sea, water shortages in the summer can be prevented. Additionally, water that has been used can be cleaned and used again to irrigate crops or top off the levels of rivers.

Collecting water when it rains is an important exercise, whether it is in a reservoir (above) or in simple pots and containers (left).

THE CLEANING-UP PROCESS

Now, all developed countries treat waste water. Water passes through to sewage plants, where waste and chemicals are removed. The clean water is then put back into the river to be used again.

Water from the Lea River, a river running off the Thames near London in Britain, is used seven times. It has traveled through seven taps, been drunk by seven groups of people, passed through seven sewage plants, and been put back into the Lea River as clean water seven times before it flows into the Thames River and then out to the sea.

Thames Water Company checks every day to see that the river water is clean.

CASE STUDY

NEW YORK CITY

CONSERVING RESOURCES

In New York, the water company decided to replace 1.3 million toilets and a million shower heads to save water. The old toilets used 4.8 gallons of water for each flush; the new design uses only 1.6 gallons. It cost the company $250 for each new toilet, but it was quicker, cheaper, and better for the environment than building the giant new reservoir that was otherwise needed. Demand for water has gone down in New York City as a result of the changes.

Customers in New York City are very happy with their new toilets and showers, provided free of charge.

AGENDA 21 aims to:

- halt deforestation
- promote the planting of millions of new trees
- show how to use and value forest products
- encourage society to leave forest tribes in peace

Rain forests help control the climate.

CUTTING DOWN THE FORESTS

Trees are vital for many reasons. Wood from trees has been used by people over thousands of years to make life easier and more comfortable. Throughout history, wood has been a main building material. It is also used to provide heat to keep us warm and for cooking.

"National action programs to plant trees and allow damaged forests to regrow should be established."

AGENDA 21

Although concrete and steel are now widely used, wood still forms part or all of many buildings throughout the world.

Trees provide food and shelter. Hundreds of trees together make a forest. When it rains on forests, water soaks into leaves, roots, and fallen debris. The water leaks out gradually into streams and rivers. By holding back rainwater in this way, trees help to stop flooding. As water evaporates from forests, clouds form and create rain in other places.

LIVING AND BREATHING

Trees help keep the air we breathe from becoming too polluted. Trees live by taking carbon dioxide from the air, using sunlight, and taking food from the soil. Carbon dioxide is a gas, but trees turn it into a form of solid carbon in order to grow. Forests help prevent global warming by storing surplus carbon dioxide. While doing all this good work, trees also make oxygen and release it into the air. Humans and animals use oxygen to breathe and stay alive. In turn, they breathe out carbon dioxide.

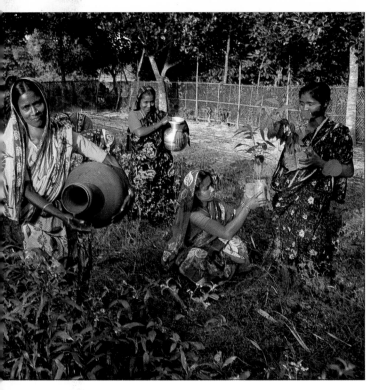

Because trees are so important, there are many projects to protect and grow them. Here, women tend a tree nursery in Bangladesh.

CASE STUDY

SOUTH AMERICA

FARMING THE FOREST

In South America, experts have learned that keeping an acre of trees is more valuable than cutting the trees down and turning the land over to cattle for grazing. Fruit gathered in the forest can be sold, vines can be used to make rope, sap from trees can be collected to make rubber for car tires. All of this means managing the forest carefully to produce several crops at once. It is called farming the forest and is an example of sustainable use.

As well as providing valuable products, trees prevent desertification by holding soil together with their roots.

DISAPPEARING FORESTS

Once, most of the world's land surface was covered in trees. For thousands of years, however, people have been clearing trees to obtain wood for building and fuel and to provide land on which to grow crops or graze sheep and cattle.

"The traditional homes and lifestyles of forest dwelling peoples should be preserved."

AGENDA 21

The destruction of the rain forest is happening at a great speed.

Yanomami tribal farmers of the Venezuelan Amazon live in harmony with their environment.

In the last 50 years, forests have been cut down at an alarming rate. While the demand for wood has grown, farmers, too, have cleared forests in order to get more land. The homes of many plants and animals have disappeared, and people from forest-dwelling tribes have been driven from their villages.

Deforestation has also altered the climate — in some places it no longer rains, and farmers have lost their land to spreading deserts.

In Washington State, in the United States, the destruction of the rain forest is plain to see.

A FUTURE AIM

Europe was once covered in forests; now four-fifths of the continent is covered in cities, farms, roads, and barren land. All countries in Europe are now planting new trees. Britain, with only 5% of its land area covered in trees (the smallest percentage of any country in Europe), is aiming to double its number of trees by 2050.

Ninety-four percent of the world's remaining forests is still unprotected from being cut down.

Once forested, much of the British countryside is now farmland.

CASE STUDY

ACROSS THE GLOBE

MANAGING THE FORESTS

The World Wide Fund for Nature, together with other environmental groups, timber traders, foresters, and stores, has begun the Forest Stewardship Council (FSC) to encourage good forest management worldwide. It awards a special FSC label to products made from wood that comes from forests where the environment and the local people are being taken care of. Where products show the FSC logo, shoppers can identify items that have been made from wood from well-managed forests.

As people become more aware of the importance of buying goods made from sustainable resources, the FSC label (shown to the right) will become more familiar.

AGENDA 21 aims to:
- save species from extinction
- study, learn from, and understand plants and animals

THE VARIETY OF LIFE

Every handful of earth and drop of water is full of life, often tiny specks that can be seen only through a microscope. Deep in forests or oceans and in the middle of deserts, there are large and small creatures alike, many yet to be discovered by people. The world is truly a wonderful place with millions of creatures, plants, and trees that have each adapted to live and thrive in different conditions. This vast range of species is called biodiversity.

All over the earth, there are different forms of life. Some plants and animals appear in many different habitats. Others may appear in only one specialized environment, such as on the desert floor.

ECOSYSTEMS

All species rely on other insects, plants, or birds in order to survive. This kind of relationship is called an ecosystem. For example, many flowers produce nectar to lure honeybees. The bees travel from flower to flower carrying pollen, a procedure necessary to fertilize these flowers. Many different types of plants and animals may be dependent on each other in this way in any ecosystem.

SURVIVAL

As populations rise and the existing countryside is put under greater pressure, more natural habitats are destroyed. Many plant and animal species are lost in this way — and it is a great loss. Different species are valuable and should be saved for their own sakes, but we can also learn from them. Many plants and animals have special properties that can be studied for human use, so it is important to preserve them.

Pandas, like many large animal species, are in danger of extinction. Smaller species, including bugs and plants, are also important but are disappearing without being noticed.

CASE STUDY

THE GREAT RAIN FORESTS
OF THE WORLD

"We need to better protect and manage ecosystems for a safer, more prosperous future."

AGENDA 21

21

VALUABLE PROPERTIES

Many drugs used in medicine today originate from herbal medicine. Aspirin comes from willow bark; codeine and morphine come from poppies. Quinine is another plant extract used in drugs all over the world to combat malaria, a disease spread by the bite of the tropical mosquito. Many Europeans visiting Africa were killed by malaria before a drug was discovered by a combination of luck, accident, and observation. It was found that the juice from the bark of a Peruvian cinchona tree both prevented and treated malaria; the juice contained quinine.

Quinine is extracted from the dried bark or trunk of the cinchona tree.

- promote the wise use of resources
- prevent the waste of fuel
- reduce pollution to protect health
- stop acid rain

VALUABLE RESOURCES

Oil, coal, and gas are found deep within the earth in many parts of the world. Now, the industries that find, dig up, and distribute these fuels create the world's biggest businesses.

Oil, mined from platforms like this one off Norway, is used for fuel and to make plastics, nylon, and other everyday items.

FUEL AND FUMES

Oil can be burned like coal but can also be refined to make gasoline and diesel fuel. One of coal's main uses is in power stations, where it is burned to make electricity. All these processes produce smoke and cause pollution.

The chemical sulfur, contained in smoke, mixes with water in the atmosphere to create sulfuric acid. This falls as acid rain and damages the environment. Some countries are now combating acid rain by taking the sulfur out of the smoke from power stations.

As the acid levels of rivers and lakes rise, plant and animal life dies.

A CLEANER FUEL

Gas is tapped from the ground and distributed in pipelines to be used for central heating, cooking, and powering factories. It is a much cleaner fuel than either coal or oil because it does not contain sulfur and other chemicals. However, just like all fossil fuels, it still produces a lot of carbon dioxide, which contributes to the problem of global warming.

Gas escapes from underground as oil is collected. Rather than use the gas, a valuable resource in itself, it is wasted by being burned.

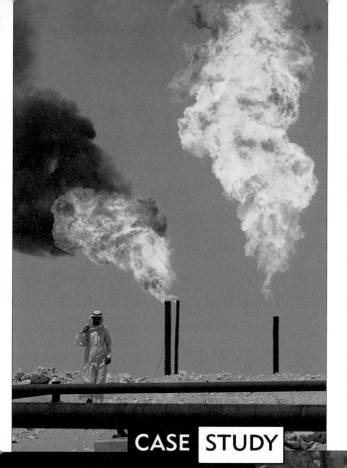

CASE STUDY

GERMANY AND INDIA

IMPROVING TECHNOLOGY, REDUCING POLLUTION

Siemans Power Generation Group of Germany formed an agreement with Gharat Heavy Electricals Ltd. of India to export the technology for highly efficient coal- and gas-driven turbines for producing electricity. The deal provided Germany with important export orders. It also provided India with technology to produce more electricity using less fuel and creating fewer harmful emissions. Both countries and both companies have gained.

Delhi, India, is a very polluted city, like many of the capitals around the world. This pollution could be reduced by using new technology.

23

WILL THEY RUN OUT?

Peat, oil, coal, and gas are all non-renewable fuels — eventually they will run out. Before that happens, the pollution caused by burning all these fuels will make life very unpleasant and cause environmental damage to the earth. World leaders have decided that it is important to cut down on burning these fuels as much as possible.

"Those who cause or threaten environmental harm should bear the full costs of controlling emissions and repairing the damage done by them."

AGENDA 21

Agenda 21 encourages governments to make companies pay for cleaning up the pollution they cause.

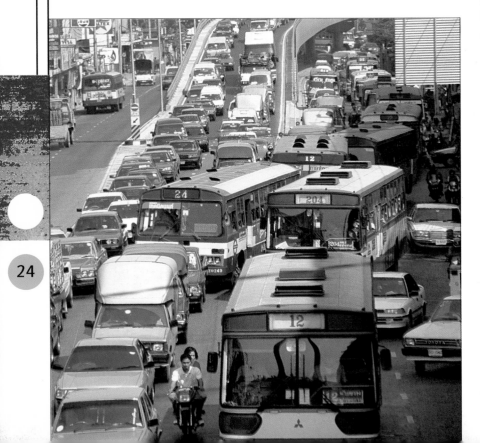

"Transportation is the fastest growing user of energy, posing major problems of traffic jams, noise, health, <u>and</u> countryside is disappearing under new roads.'

UK Electricity Association.

Cars, trucks, and buses eat up fossil fuels. Alternative forms of transportation need to be researched.

There are many ways to reduce the use of fossil fuels: cars could be produced to travel farther on less fuel, and people's homes could be better insulated so they need less gas, oil, or coal to heat them. Lightbulbs are being made that use one-fifth the electricity used by standard bulbs but produce the same brightness. It is hoped that through improvements in technology, alternative methods of fueling industry can also be found.

Solar power, the renewable energy of the future, is put to industrial use in Spain at this solar power station.

CLEANER, CHEAPER
TRANSPORTATION

Electric vehicles are on trial in several countries in Europe. At La Rochelle, France, parking places at homes and in the city center have been provided with electricity points so people can plug in and recharge the batteries in their cars while they sleep or shop. In Cologne, Germany, a similar system is being tested, but there the car batteries are powered by solar energy.

The running cost of electric cars is one-third the price of gasoline-driven cars and half the cost of cars that run on diesel fuel.

Not only is this car in Cologne run on batteries, but the batteries are powered by the sun. This saves on money as well as resources.

AGENDA 21 aims to:

- promote different forms of energy that do not cause pollution
- increase the knowledge and use of clean technology throughout the world
- promote recycling of existing resources

Recycling saves energy and resources.

ALTERNATIVE ENERGIES

WHAT IS RENEWABLE?

Coal, oil, and gas can be burned only once and then are gone forever. But the wind blows most of the year, the sun comes up every morning, and rivers flow continuously when they are fed by new rains. If these natural forces can be used to make electricity on a large scale, then energy can be constantly renewable.

"Industrial countries need to consume less resources, particularly energy, and reduce emissions. This means developing renewable energy."

AGENDA 21

The technology now exists for windmills to drive turbines. It has long been possible to make electricity from waterpower, with river currents pushing wheels. Electricity can now be produced directly from sunlight, and solar energy can also be used to heat water.

Wind farms, where wind is used to make electricity, are becoming big business in many countries.

ANOTHER ALTERNATIVE

Nuclear power was once seen as the great hope for the future. In the 1960s, the idea of producing unlimited power from tiny atoms crashing into each other captured the imagination of the world.

Since then, nuclear power has proven very expensive because it is dangerous and has to be carefully controlled. Getting rid of nuclear waste is another extremely serious problem. The waste remains damaging to human health and harms animal and plant life for thousands of years. As a result, developing nuclear power goes against many of the aims of Agenda 21 because the unsolved problems of this generation are passed on to the next.

A German worker lowers radioactive fuel rods into a special container for transporting the nuclear waste.

The oil industry, including companies like the China Petroleum Refinery in Taiwan, is one of the world's biggest employers.

COMPARING COSTS

Industries involved with the processing of oil, coal, and gas employ thousands of people. Governments are reluctant to close factories and mines, which would put many people out of work. Additionally, relying on coal, oil, and gas has previously seemed cheaper than taking on the costs of developing new technologies. However, if the cost of the pollution created by burning fossil fuels is taken into account, clean, renewable technologies are more attractive.

By increasing the production and use of wind turbines, making electricity from wind will become cheaper than making it from coal.

BACK TO THE BEGINNING

Wind, sun, wave, and tidal power are energies of the past and of the future. Building new wind farms is now cheaper than building coal-fired power stations. The price of electricity generated by the sun through solar panels is still very high but is falling as more of the special solar panels are made. Producing such panels will soon be big business too.

"Renewable energy sources were for millions of years the only sources of energy for life on Earth.
This will happen again in the near future."

Hermann Scheer,
President of Eurosolar, 1997.

CASE STUDY

SWITZERLAND

SOLAR POWER

Global warming is a very real threat. In Switzerland it is causing glaciers to melt and less snow to fall in the winter. This affects the country's tourist trade, because the skiing season is cut short. In turn, this affects Switzerland's wealth. The government decided to promote the use of solar energy in order to cut carbon dioxide emissions and reduce global warming. Already 43 school projects to install solar panels are under way. Many schools are producing more electricity than they need.

By selling the "free" surplus electricity, the Swiss schools are not only providing a non-polluting energy source but are also making a profit.

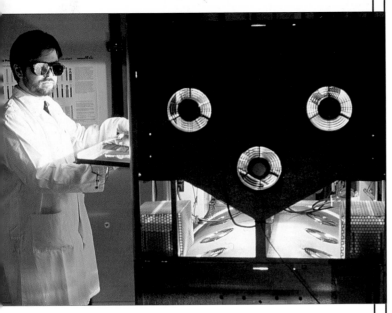

British scientists experiment to perfect photovoltaic cells so they can produce electricity as cheaply as possible.

RENEWABLE AND REUSABLE

Solar power is considered to be the future source for providing electricity. Photovoltaic cells, used to collect the sun's energy, have the advantage that they can be set up anywhere and produce electricity instantly without any pollution. This is valuable for people in poor countries with no electricity at all at present.

"Renewable energy currently provides 2% of the world's supplies. A vast expansion is needed to meet energy needs in the next century."

World Energy Council report, 1996.

Scientists today are working on wave and tidal power. The technology works but is still expensive. Together, renewable sources of energy could provide enough power for the whole world and bring pollution down to a fraction of the current level.

People can help save our world's resources by using renewable sources of energy as they become available. The more people who use them, the cheaper they will become. By combining renewable energies with the careful recycling of existing materials, we will move closer to becoming a sustainable society.

As renewable energy sources, such as tidal power, become more widely available, they will also become less expensive.

GLOSSARY

atoms: tiny particles that make up all matter. Splitting atoms releases huge power and heat.

ban: when an activity is not allowed by law or official rules.

biodiversity: the variety of plant and animal life.

cultivate: to prepare soil in order to grow food crops.

dam: a barrier built across a river to hold back the water.

deforestation: cutting down or destroying trees to use the wood or turn the forests into farmland.

developed country: a country that relies on money from industry and in which factories provide more jobs than agriculture.

developing country: a country that relies on agriculture, rather than on manufacturing goods for export, for example.

ecosystem: the network of animals and plants that interact with and depend on each other in a particular area.

emissions: smoke, gases, liquids, or other substances left over after industrial processing. For example, the smoke caused by burning coal to make electricity is an emission.

energy: the power that is needed to create activity or movement. For example, fossil fuels are burned to create heat, which can be used to power an engine.

evaporates: when a solid or liquid is turned into a gas; for example, when water is heated, it evaporates into steam.

fertile: productive or fruitful. Fertile soil is rich in goodness and so produces excellent crops.

irrigate: to artificially water crops.

non-renewable: something that cannot be replaced. Once a non-renewable resource, such as oil, is taken from the environment, it is gone permanently.

ozone layer: ozone is a special gas, including oxygen, that is in the atmosphere. A layer of the gas about 13 miles to 16 miles (20 kilometers to 25 kilometers) above the earth's surface acts as a barrier to harmful rays from the sun.

renewable: something that can be replaced or regrown, for example, trees; or a source of energy that never runs out, such as the sun or wind.

reservoir: an artificial or natural lake that stores water.

resources: a stock or supply of a material.

sanitation: the provision of toilets and washing facilities to help people keep clean and to dispose of sewage.

species: the different family groups of animals.

sustainable: in this instance, to be able to maintain lifestyles or preserve resources over a long period of time.

turbines: a motor or machine driven by water, steam, or gas to create energy or electricity.

virus: tiny disease-producing agents that cause colds and other illnesses.

FURTHER INFORMATION

American Petroleum Institute
1220 L Street, NW
Washington, DC 20005
(202) 682-8000

EarthAction International
30 Cottage Street
Amherst, MA 01002
(413) 549-8118

Earthwatch
680 Mt. Auburn Street
Box 403
Watertown, MA 02272
(617) 926-8200

Energy Frontiers International
1110 N. Glebe Road
Suite 610
Arlington, VA 22201
(703) 276-6655

Environmental and Energy Studies Institute
122 C Street
Suite 700
Washington, DC 20001
(202) 628-1400

Natural Resources Defense Council
40 W. 20th Street
New York, NY 10011
(212) 727-2700

Sierra Club National Headquarters
85 2nd Street
San Francisco, CA 94101
(415) 977-5500

U.S. Department of Energy
1000 Independence Avenue, SW
Washington, DC 20585
(202) 586-5000

INDEX